FOUR POINTS FOURTEEN LINES

FOUR POINTS
FOURTEEN LINES

EYEWEAR PUBLISHING

TONY CHAN

First published in 2016
by Eyewear Publishing Ltd
Suite 333, 19-21 Crawford Street
Marylebone, London W1H 1PJ
United Kingdom

Cover design and typeset by Edwin Smet
Author photograph by Soho Print Store
Map illustration by Charles Wentworth-Stanley
Printed in England by TJ International Ltd, Padstow, Cornwall

ISBN 978-1-911335-17-7

*Eyewear wishes to thank Jonathan Wonham for his
generous patronage of our press.*

WWW.EYEWEARPUBLISHING.COM

For my parents, who were there for my first steps.

THE
MELITA HUME
POETRY PRIZE

Tony Chan is a 2015 winner
of the Melita Hume Poetry Prize. He received
£750 and this publication by Eyewear Publishing.
The 2015 Judge was Toby Martinez de las Rivas.
His citation read:

Tony Chan's *Four Points Fourteen Lines*
has a remarkable back-story. In January this year,
Tony left his job, and embarked on a 78-day, 1,400-mile trek
across Britain, incorporating its northern, southern, western and eastern
extremities. That in itself is an extraordinary undertaking, but Tony also
produced a sonnet at the end of each day – these sonnets constituted the
collection, each one unedited and presented entirely as it emerged on the
day in question. Tony has reached into the past and brought us a new way of
seeing an old, familiar form, and he has done it with skill. Looking back over my
notes as I was reading the collection, I find the following: 'Supremely generous',
'At times, technically brilliant', 'A clever mix of overblown Romantic structures
with a self-deprecating tone which is very attractive'. It is undoubtedly not
perfect – he often writes in full rhyme, and iambic pentameter, fantastically
difficult to control even with forensic editing – but that slight unevenness
is all part of the fun, part of the hugely generous vision,
the willingness to push on, which makes this collection
ultimately so rewarding and enjoyable.

Table of Contents

Explanatory Note

The following poems were composed on each day of a
78-day, 1,400-mile solo-trek between the four extreme
cardinal points of the British mainland. The walk began
on 3 January, 2015, at the northernmost point, Dunnet
Head, continuing on to Ardnamurchan Point and
Lowestoft Ness, before finishing at Lizard Point.

Apart from minor corrections, each poem remains
unimproved from the day on which it was first written.

Route Map

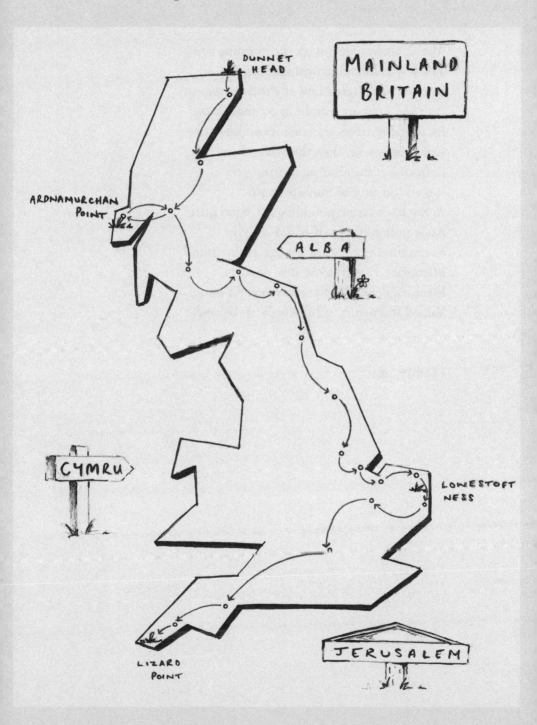

Dunnet Head to Wick

Ahead, at shoulders with the morning mist,
The way is lit and temptingly begun
By cloud-splintered rays of the dawning sun:
Path and light are caught in conjugal kiss.
Excitement drives the eager heart onward –
One foot works, then the other of the pair,
In front lies the alluring morning air.
It is all too easy to move forward.
At my back arrive poundings of wind gust
Aside pummellings of hail. I pace on,
Feet stamping forward yet against my mind.
Memories distant decay into dust,
Memories cherished are too soon far gone:
Valued fragments of life lived, left behind.

3 January, 2015

Wick to Dunbeath

It is Sunday. The retail park on the
Grey edge of town calls with frenetic hum;
A pound-beast, which daily trolls for the thrum
Of commerce and the throng of consumers.
All else is shut in these rural outlands
Of forgotten villages and nameless
Hamlets: the churches are closed and lifeless
Amidst empty homes flagged by 'For Sale' stands.
Where might the weary search for food and rest?
There, near, a couple waits at their front door
With welcome arms and kind offers of tea,
Cheese rolls and crisps; then for every guest,
Respite and company, mirth and much more.
Let there still be light for all who can see.

4 January, 2015

Dunbeath to Helmsdale

Go be enlightened! Find your Nirvana!
Empowerment! Yes! Self-actualise!
Remember when you wished upon a star?
Hold fast to your dreams! Reach up for the skies!
Hell, why not take on a pilgrimage too?
Perambulation and isolation –
It's really quite a simple thing to do.
Yes! There's your perfect mid-life solution!
Self-help words: vacuous as hollow reeds,
All false prophets of Chi and Karmic flows.
Something else tends to guide our lives instead:
An acceptance of Maslow's basic needs.
Whatever one thinks, wherever one goes,
There's the daily hunt for bog, bath and bed.

5 January, 2015

Helmsdale to Golspie

The boy, whatever happened to the boy?
The one who lived through the stories he read
Whilst dreamfully asleep upon his bed:
For whom a book meant more than any toy.
Beyond the mind with Barrie's Pan he flew,
And through New York with Holden Caulfield strode.
He found freedom out on Kerouac's road,
And acted Bond for just one day, or two.
The man steps out from his long-mortgaged home,
Ready to face, in his brown worsted suit,
The adventure of the daily commute:
He tap-taps away on his mobile phone.
Does the boy still call within the man's heart?
Enough to lead towards another start?

6 January, 2015

Golspie to Tain

Things were pleasant at starting. Suddenly
Comes an Old Testament of deluge and
Tempest, deluding the senses wholly
And tempting curse-words at Heaven's hard hand.
Hood up, head bowed, teeth-at-grit and eyes steeled,
Fighting drunken swings of the wind's attack,
I advance with thighs tensed and shoulder dropped,
Bull-headedly forward, not looking back.
Here, upon the bridge astride Dornoch Firth,
Iced rain cannoned by fast-rasping wind flies
With scream and haunt, and (for what it is worth)
Leaves a sting of pinpricks around my eyes.
Twelve hundred miles still left for me to plod:
A mile-long bridge shows simply how great is God.

7 January, 2015

Tain to Evanton

Yesterday I wrote a poem about God
Then sent it out for the whole world to read
And there has been no protest no dissent
The lines remain unchanged and unchanging
Today I collect the news one day late
Despite the distance there is emotion
A sense of some shared human connection
And thoughts on the virtues of tolerance
Tomorrow I shall walk again and breathe
Through the fresh-cut crop fields of Cromarty
An entire expanse still to be explored
Full of possibilities and futures
Time spins the wheel of sorrow and healing
Not all things are unchanged

Je suis Charlie

8 January, 2015

Evanton to Inverness

Behold that metropolis, master-planned
In neatly drawn cell-blocks of cinema
Multiplexes and multi-storey car
Parks, beside green spaces where booze is banned
(The same at the square that ensnares the hair
Salon between a brace of guardsman bars);
All bounded by dual-carriageways of cars,
Hurried and held between home and elsewhere.
A calmed river leads out from the centre
To an ancient lake where monsters once ran,
With its long shores of neglected mooring
Where boats float in wait for a visitor:
The city is a prison built by man,
A subconscious enclosure of blinding.

9 January, 2015

Inverness to Foyers

O shoes! Impermeable by water,
You loyally guard my feet, heel-to-toe.
I'll never forget our miles together:
Us? We'll always have Kilimanjaro.
Beloved *makhila*, twinned stick and weapon,
Hewn from medlar by a Basque magician.
With strength you carry my weight and burden:
By my side, my most trusted companion.
And you, lycra undershorts, with your snug
Support and warm comfort through the long haul,
Caressing my thighs with your constant hug:
You know me most intimately of all.
Wait – I'm making friends with objects – maybe
This week on foot has driven me crazy.

10 January, 2015

Foyers to Invergarry

I've had a tough day at the office. Rain
And sharp-angled winds dashed down the mountains:
Who needs Kitzbühel when such a menace show
Of menace snow boxes the blunt body?
Pressed-down I pushed on and pressed the body
To hold its warmth by shouting out old show
Tunes to an audience of white mountains,
Which clapped back thunder and rapacious rain.
What else might be unearthed at the office?
Violent threat, financial trouble, ill health:
Countless others must endure even worse.
Perspective. I'm blessed not to counter worse.
Today's been full fun and I'm high on health:
I've not had a tough day at the office.

11 January, 2015

Invergarry to Spean Bridge

The wrong people get all the attention.
Whereas Hector, horse-breaker, stands for Troy
Through selfless severance from wife and boy,
Achilles courts the critics' affection.
An angst of Achilles begins the book
With violence and vengeance and brooding breath;
The epic ends rightly at Hector's death
– No more story – the hero's life forsook.
Something of high-honourable Hector
Subsists in the people of these Highlands:
Something sincere in their browned, moss-green tweeds,
In their greeting voice of gentle tenor.
From ancient Hector or from ancient clans,
Here live men most earnest in words and deeds.

12 January, 2015

Spean Bridge to Corran

Sunday coming marks my mother's birthday –
Sixty years of her loves and labours shared.
My web-order jewels reach Sydney today –
Substitution for my own presence there.
We divorced at that change: young man to man –
She cried then, cries now, with the same hurt heart.
A hollow: one Chan and one other Chan –
Each lives a life a hemisphere apart.
This night, I stand at water's edge and stare
Across the loch to a strange relation.
The surname is shared, but not so the rare
And real love of a mother's devotion.
I think of sons, of given, of taken,
And stare no longer at Ardnamurchan.

13 January, 2015

Note: The start of the Ardnamurchan peninsula sits opposite Corran, across Loch Linnhe. Ardnamurchan Point is situated at the westernmost end of the peninsula.

Corran to Resipole

There have been holidays of expensive
Taste and expanding waist, well beyond my
Means of credit; and sojourns more pensive
And private, sight-seeing with soul, then eye.
Rome, Santiago, The Cipriani
For dinner, South Pacific, Eurasia
By road to Samarkand, Bern, Brittany,
Sylt, Niagara, the top of Africa.
Now a modest pauper of meagre plans,
A wanderer of indefinite place;
On foot, by chance and through grace, I happen
To stumble upon the most wondrous land
In all the known worlds of wild time and space.
Forget Paris. Come find Ardnamurchan.

14 January, 2015

Resipole to Kilchoan

Another's words might write up what I see
Far West on the West Coast of the Highlands:
There are the 'sun-dappled native woodlands'
That *Lonely Planet* picture-paints for me;
Rough Guides goes geeky on geography,
Making good mention of the 'wild and bleak'
Rock-cliff forms, and speaks of a well-spent week
In 'starkly beautiful' topography;
The *Official Website* simply describes
This spot as the 'perfect destination';
Whilst short breaks in a 'remote' location
Are what Dr. *Visit Scotland* prescribes.
What are the *mots justes* which may justly set
Something beyond words into a sonnet?

15 January, 2015

Kilchoan to Ardnamurchan Point to Kilchoan

There were times, at bedtime, when my daddy
Told the one lonely tale that he knew best,
The sino-story, *Journey to the West*,
With its magi heroes, Monk and Monkey.
Here I stand, having chased my father's voice,
Rock under my feet, waves against the rock,
And waves all through the line of nine o'clock:
At journey's end, there is only one choice.
I revolve around and roll the steps back
Through the path and through moments in my mind:
Regret, not compass, dictates direction.
All that I once did appears on the track,
Alongside all that I once wished to find.
Eastward I walk, in prayerful oblation.

16 January, 2015

Kilchoan to Resipole

What do you presume of a B&B?
Dream-soft bedding on a wonder-soft bed?
Books of real appeal to both heart and head?
A chocolate box choice of black and green teas?
Perchance a sea-view of yet unseen hope?
Delectable hunks of home-baked delights?
Bells-and-whistles heating and stylish lights?
Luxury bath with luxurious soap?
I have stayed somewhere of more and better,
Not more of things but of things substantial:
A cathedral window that stirs the soul;
Comfort and care for a wearied walker;
Hosts humble and kind and each an angel;
All found at *Rockpool House* in Resipole.

17 January, 2015

Resipole to Corran

Health check: there's a superficial gash on
The back of my left calf, and my left foot
Is a tad tender at the top tendon.
Extensor tendonitis: simply put
Right with rest. Otherwise, the body's fine.
I suppose I'm quite steady mentally:
I talk, *ma tête à ma tête*, all the time,
But I'm still some steps from insanity.
My spirit? It's revived in this Eden,
Cradled in the hand of The Almighty.
I ask and seek and knock, all to Heaven,
And walk on in penitent piety.
Three hundred and one-point-nine miles now done;
For Suffolk, six hundred miles more to come.

18 January, 2015

Corran to Kingshouse

I have met all sorts on the road so far:
First was the drunk granddad, Old Pulteney,
Nursed by his carer, Al Ness. 'He's a star',
Said neighbours, both Glens (Mhor and Morangie).
Out West, the public schoolboy twins, Garry
And Gordon Inver, rods in hand, were taught
To cast by their uncles (military
Majors) William and Augustus Fort.
Plainly, I have not met many women
Aside from a most fleeting flirtation
With that mysterious island girl, Skye.
The state of play may change next week, and I
Dream of some chance to unclip Helen's Burgh,
After we meet for drinks at the Dun Bar.

19 January, 2015

Kingshouse to Crianlarich

Acres of moors wear blankets of hoary
Flakes beneath a sky of dove-grey billow,
Flanked by rough-hewn hills coloured with wintry
Pastels washed through this *blanc de blancs* tableau.
Odd and dotted, above the fresh fall of
Snow, several defiant conifers
Have pushed through their pustule tops: brushes of
Tar in an arctic of alabaster.
A scuttle of rust-red deer fleet-foots through,
Transient for a ticking moment: gone.
Low in the valley, the lake is iced blue
Faint-tinted, underneath the soft-bleached sun.
Nothing is here of the manners of men,
Only of manna sent down from heaven.

20 January, 2015

Crianlarich to Tarbet

Carcasses sag on the roads as remains
Decayed to skeletal shapes, or riven
Asunder to display red-ripe swollen
Innards slowly seeping new asphalt stains.
They were not to know the laws that dictate
Momentum and inclement instances
And increases in braking distances:
And thus they came to face their fall and fate.
Ecce homo, me, just an animal
Rambling the roads in a frenzied flurry
To duck obese-laden lorries that pass
Suddenly with speed and without signal,
Saved by my lane-leap and verge-hop scurry.
What good is *sapiens* in a carcass?

21 January, 2015

Tarbet to Balloch

Something is new-found to the time before:
The resting water soundless-still, kissing
Inaudibly on the hulls of loose-moored
Pleasure crafts, each smooth-muted peck touching
In step with the fall of my feet onto
The loch-shore path, full-suffused by serene
Crepuscular light, each shadow forms new
Soft-shapes waiting to be both sensed and seen.
A decade has run since I was here last
And this here is now a different place.
Then, I was hastening south to Glasgow,
And Lomond unobserved as I drove past
With uncaring glance at rental car pace,
Rash-rushing around what I did not know.

22 January, 2015

Balloch to Strathblane

An arrow points the way – a direction
Marked out for herds of cyclists and walkers
And odd packs of ultra-marathoners,
Who follow the bright-signed indication
Absorbed in athletic recreation,
Full-clothed in air-wove fluorescent sweaters
Adorned with luminescent reflectors –
A shepherd's signal for the next station.
The mind, unbound, unchained from dutiful
Navigation, wills to waft and wander
Through yawning floods of thought both wrought and rife
With memory, settles at a single
Sudden, when meditations meander
By higher way, of higher truth and life.

23 January, 2015

Strathblane to Falkirk

Specials boards are burst and crowded with game:
Venison steaks, venison casseroles,
Some quail, some grouse, then venison again,
Twice-diced, fine-minced or rolled as small rissoles.
Pubs market their menus of freshly-made,
Inanely variant burger patties;
And hawk that staple of the tourist trade,
Ubiquitous haggis, neeps and tatties.
The game's afoot for the non-meat-eater;
Yet, there's a dish for the discerning taste,
Which all vegetarians ought to try.
One pie shell, cheap cheese and cheap pack pasta
– A trinity conjoined in congealed paste –
Baked then plated as Macaroni Pie.

24 January, 2015

Falkirk to South Queensferry

What a strange beast, the regional high street:
Boarded-up, malnourished and neglected,
It's a civic species much endangered.
Those vital organs matured incomplete:
No butcher, no baker, no blankmonger;
Merely thrift-aid shops and chains to lay bets
And a surfeit of signs, 'For Sale or Let'.
The supermarket has proved the victor.
Yet glitz and size faces its own demise,
Threatened by more intelligent design
That barks, bites, brings the market primate down:
Online the merchants roar in evolved guise.
In coming time will there be welcome signs
At each 'Historic *Super*market Town'?

25 January, 2015

South Queensferry to Edinburgh

A forward momentum defines the past
Twenty-four days out on the open road,
Four-hundred-and-fifty-nine miles of vast
Movement and daily different abode.
Motion is progress as both feet press on,
Passing by strangers with greetings polite,
Advancing towards a destination
Ahead and beyond the far edge of sight.
My shadow has come with me all the way:
A share of me, unshakeable, behind;
A spectre of experience remained.
Tonight, first time in all these walking days,
I meet old friends who know me, know my mind.
'In walking', they will ask, 'what passed, what gained?'

26 January, 2015

Edinburgh to North Berwick

Far, far in backdrop, small as a doll's house,
Is the King's castle: but our tale takes place
Down on Princes Street, where four heroes face
The world and its worst, despite their dormouse
Size. One pulls from his pouch a plastic toy,
A miniature lightsaber, transparent,
Which he lifts to his mouth like a parent-
Gifted lollipop and sucks-through with joy,
Before blowing forth bubbles of smoky
Cloud rings like working model-train chimneys.
The others follow suit, drawing with ease
From their own stash of vaporised candy.
Such are the twelve-year-old boys of today:
Death-sticks exchanged for vape and vapist play.

27 January, 2015

North Berwick to Dunbar

Today I can smell the sharp-salted breeze,
Which rhumba-steps inland from the North Sea.
Distinctive is the gritted scent that it
Leaves: an aroma familiar to
Me. It is perhaps a near-fortnight back
Since I last felt this same brackish freshness;
From the Atlantic, out on the West Coast
Track, but that tactile memory is strong
Nonetheless. I have slalomed coast-to-coast
For a second time on my month's journey:
East-to-West and now back to an eastern
Post, in driving test zigzags all down the
Country. I have charted a winding way,
Maybe a mirror to all my life's days.

28 January, 2015

Dunbar to Eyemouth

No day begins without new discomfort.
Nothing of deadly serious degree,
Simply insufficient recovery
From the daily tenders of pain and hurt:
Sore here; tight there; other niggles somewhere;
A fresh ache in those first footsteps between
Bed and bath; a strain suffered yet unseen;
Recurrent corporeal wear-and-tear.
These ailments variably appear then
Quickly disappear; a moment's nuisance
Claiming momentary acquiescence
Of body, soon repaired and unbeaten.
Rooted wounds of the unsung soul and steeled
Heart endure beyond flesh, and do not heal.

29 January, 2015

Eyemouth to Belford

Last night I slumbered under Scottish stars;
Today my eyes look on an English sky.
It is an open border, full of cars
That drown through the sound of a soft-breathed sigh.
In passing here, I leave flowered Scotland,
Leave the brave company of Scots wha hae,
Yearning to pray again at this Highland
Cathedral with remembrance of past days.
Further south rise broad mountains, green with pines,
Sat silently above pleasant pastures
Of the free and freed; and onward of them,
A distant sea of clouded hills entwines
A nation's dreams to mythical futures.
Farewell, Alba. Welcome, Jerusalem.

30 January, 2015

Belford to Alnwick

That is it. No more of rock-ridged mountains
Nor remote wilds of nature's best beauty;
No stretch of troubling solitude remains.
All are gone. The way ahead is easy:
In front stands modern civilisation,
A network of neighboured towns and cities
Heavy and heaving with population
And roads that run to shops from factories.
Gone as well is the spirit of challenge,
The grand illusion of bold adventure,
The grave fear of the near-impossible,
From which the resolute soul can scavenge
Out of the depths, hope and redemption sure.
What satisfaction is without struggle?

31 January, 2015

Alnwick to Morpeth

A skein of geese above with drumming wings,
The hourglass that lets slip the sands of time,
The course of sun through giant cyclic rings,
A loop unfurling from the smooth-cast line,
A mechanic song of sliding pistons,
The ebb and the flow of the moon-pulled tides,
The pulse from ventricle to atrium,
A sinusoid shaped in carousel rides,
A balletic spin of the lighthouse lamp,
The rise and fall of the resting torso,
The slower shuffle of waltzing soft-stamp,
A baton floated by the old maestro:
And so it is with man and his own feet,
That each walking step tends the rhythmic beat.

1 February, 2015

Morpeth to Newcastle

Down the road from the demolition site
Sits a worn row of shops; feeble lamplight
Fails to illuminate the full-framed height
Of the murky windows. Caught in a fight
Outside, a drunkard, with both fists clenched tight,
Labours to thrash the air in his upright
Boxing stance, whilst he spits out impolite
Spills of words with blustered and bitter bite.
This is a dimmed and dulled place, and despite
All the promise of better life at night
Time, nothing here has managed to ignite
My heart, quicken the weakened pulse, excite
The mind. I find that I have nought to write
Of its tasteless, non-existent delight.

2 February, 2015

Newcastle to Durham

Running to bed with much rushed excitement
Was once the highlight of my holidays:
Nothing else could charm with such enchantment
As the upper bunk on nights spent away.
They were the best of all bedtime moments:
A monkey's scamper up the ladder bars,
Then wholesome rest with soul and mind content,
At sleep a few feet closer to the stars.
Last night I was so suddenly older,
My selection made swiftly and complete.
I opted for the alternative love,
Tempted by that other bunk – the lower –
With its ease-of-access and makeshift seat,
And view towards the vacant bed above.

3 February, 2015

Durham to Darlington

Spaced apart are the twenty customers
Sat in this brand-name coffee concession,
Armchairs are set at face to each other
But each sits in quiet desperation.
That man reads his book, those three fiddle phones,
Two type on tablets in dull distraction;
All are connected to a thing alone
And inured to absent conversation.
As I stand to leave, a girl looks at me,
With all she hopes to say still yet unheard.
My eyes meet hers as they lift from the floor:
I smile, shyly; she smiles back, equally.
Neither she nor I speak a single word
Before I turn towards the exit door.

4 February, 2015

Darlington to Northallerton

There is a tune I learnt and sang at school,
Of affecting antipodean truth.
My heart has carried its music in full,
Ever since those halcyon days of youth.
Now grown and distant in a foreign land,
Childhood seems a memory kept far back.
I travel light, with my stick held in hand,
And all that I own shouldered in my pack.
As I walk, wayfarer in nature's host,
I hear, singing out from the southern seas,
The question of that jolly swagman's ghost,
'Who'll come a-waltzing Matilda, with me?'
Though I have danced wide and far through Britain,
I have never been more Australian.

5 February, 2015

Northallerton to Easingwold

Trains rupture the calm of drifting daydreams,
Sounding a harsh wake of high-speed hurtle;
Passengers within snooze and stare at screens,
Oblivious to the grinding rattle.
Cars wail unpredictable engine tones,
Erratic between speed-up and slow-down;
Drivers fix their eyes on sat-navs and phones,
Muddled by a messy rat-run through town.
Cycles pass with less speed but greater haste,
Riders breathe out in exhausted octaves;
Focused on minimal energy waste,
They firmly pedal past without a wave.
To walk is slower than bike, car and rail:
But slow enough to notice some detail.

6 February, 2015

Easingwold to York

Much time has been spent on the road walking,
Counting up the many miles covered through
Accumulation of steps, and thinking
Of where it all began. What things are new,
And what existed before the start? I
Know where I have come from; a past once grey
In mind has resolved clear as clearest sky:
Now here I am, at the point of halfway.
Things change and it comes time to consider
Where life leads in the strange miles beyond the
Finish. Counting down both distance and days,
What waits at that moment of encounter
With zero? Does clarity light the blur
Of sundry destinies that end the way?

7 February, 2015

York to Selby

It is opening hour and the shops wait
With wantage of early-morning browsers.
Staff polish floors in want of customers
Who are wont to begin their shopping late.
Yet what is wanted, money or shoppers?
Windows are lined with unwanted sale stock,
Which stores are wanting to clear in bulk blocks –
Trading goods for modern seawant dollars.
I find there is nothing I wish to buy
– Content simply to stroll on nonchalant
And dismissive of both impulse and greed –
Life holds greater and grander stuffs to try.
Do we ever really need what we want,
Or inverted, want what we really need?

8 February, 2015

Selby to Thorne

A hatchback slows past a school's gated span.
At its wheel steers a driver come of age:
A boy, first-tasting life as a young man,
Dressed in the best suit of his young man's wage.
He drives all day, some place to another;
Routine errands tasked by his employment.
Once done, he motors his company car
Onwards to his next scheduled appointment.
That first licence seemed a key for free flight
From the confines of young adult life; paired
With a car, he could dream of anywhere.
Behind him, in the mid-morning dream-light,
Children spring around a playing ground, scared
Of nothing and still full of foolish dare.

9 February, 2015

Thorne to Gainsborough

I have travelled through plenteous places
And seen some who live shamed, unhappy lives;
Seen others in better circumstances,
Happy few for whom something good survives
– Something satisfactory, suitable –
Well enough with their yearly bonuses
To carry on content and comfortable,
Winning modest glories and successes.
Any quest to seek for the something more
Begins with a rejection of the old:
Acceptance that grows from humility.
There are mysterious blessings in store
For those cast-away from the daily, cold
Existence that frames the ordinary.

10 February, 2015

Gainsborough to Lincoln

'Seriously, you're walking to Lincoln?
It's probably seventeen miles, you know;
And if you're asking for my opinion,
Well, I'd go the road for Kexby, then Stow.'
'This pavement doesn't go all the way then,
Alongside this main road? Which way's quicker
And easier walking? Thank you, again,
For your time and knowledge. I'm grateful, sir.'
'Look, Lincoln is that way [*pointing left*], but
This road we're on, turns away [*pointing right*].
Best of luck: the B-road to Kexby, cut
Through Burton, and you'll have Lincoln in sight.'
'Righty-o, I'll follow your directions:
Kexby next, on your recommendation.'

11 February, 2015

Lincoln to Woodhall Spa

Il fiume scorre serpeggiante
Dalle colline all'ampio mare,
Porta via il tempo per pensare
Di tutto ed anche di niente.
L'orologio gira lentamente
Con possibilità di sperare
Per il meglio, di aspettare
Per una promessa importante.
Un potere fuori del tempo
Rende la vita miracolosa,
In tutte le sue cose belle.
Mentre i giorni diminuiscono,
Devo trovare l'unica cosa
Che move il sole e l'altre stelle.

12 February, 2015

Woodhall Spa to Boston

He who sits on the spirit of a cliff,
She who succours with her wounded nectar,
They who reign the ramparts flaunting a stiff
And most strangely erubescent flower.
One who denies the charlatan daily,
Another who feeds llamas with ashes,
Some who dance with profligate gaiety
Then croak in parsimonious flashes.
Men who barter away tramlines for tears,
Women who sing to silvered forks and spoons,
Children who scold cold incipient fears
With the warble of elegiac tunes.

My imagined stories of those inside
All the hushed house windows I pass beside.

13 February, 2015

Boston to Holbeach

I greet them politely; returned to me
Are wild grimaces of confrontation
Fronting savage stares of disaffection,
Foully hazed in violent effrontery.
They make howl in vicious and troubling key
To signal their brute-forceful aggression,
And lurk fiercely in ganged indignation,
Embittered by civil society.
Though *Manners Makyth Man* may well be true,
All pleasantries are absent around here:
But if all your life has been rotted rough,
Stolen and broken and spat back at you,
No wonder that what you know now is fear,
Faintly veiled by this play of feigning tough.

14 February, 2015

Holbeach to King's Lynn

There are times during the course of the day
When Dylan and Garfunkel sound in my
Ear, and times near to the end of the day
At which passing people ask after my
Journey; a roulette of company to
Join the bank of messages that waits on
My email server, which I reply to
Before the next day calls me to walk on.
There is no denying that these voices
And faces are all fleeting, there for a
Moment then gone; I am again lonely
In small talk with only my own voices,
Making those singular hours spent on a
Long road seem interminably lonely.

15 February, 2015

King's Lynn to Huntstanton

'You doing this for charity?' asks the
Kindly merchant, who predictably starts
With the one query always asked of me.
Is this how our world now lessens our hearts?
That anything, which carries or invents
A small aspect of surprising venture,
Demands both willpower and wonderment
Amidst unforeseen human endeavour,
Is seen possible only through prepared
Objectives of charitable giving,
Approved rational under some declared
Auspices of goodwill and fundraising?
'No, it's entirely selfish', I reply,
'A wish to live, before life passes by'.

16 February, 2015

Huntstanton to Wells-next-the-Sea

Still, my heart: it may be but a mirage,
For no earthly scene paints of such delight
So passion and reason equal excite,
Nor frames such forms of beauteous visage.
Real and present it shows, as graced light falls
By angelic lume, whilst the Zephyr's toss
Floats with cooled relief and bears far across
Shifted tides those sonorous Siren calls.
Yet clouds shade, winds twist, sounds taper empty,
And the reverie cannot be reprised.
All is departed without permanence;
Banished to lands of hollowed memory,
Not seen nor heard again, never revived,
Slips a moment of elapsed transcendence.

17 February, 2015

Wells-next-the-Sea to Cromer

I am out early this morning, setting
Off under dawned light still cold, and quick to
Rupture the steadied stillness that rests through
The saltmarsh by my purposeful marching
In resolute steps. With a glimpse behind,
I perceive that I leave the first footprints
Of today, on paths else untrod and mint,
Much like those two diverged roads of Frost's mind.
Somewhere and sometime further down the tracks
Are older impressions, pressed from a day
Before or days before then; all outlines
Of manifold treads, sole shapes and heeled backs:
My being is purely a part that plays
Within some greater song, not wholly mine.

18 February, 2015

Cromer to Wayford Bridge

Each day brings its distinct scenes and events,
Yet one thing repeats under each day's sun,
Typically with five miles still left to run:
A daily constant mid the changed moments.
As the road signs count the last stop nearer,
Though the end is not yet in sight, in mind
Is always the same tired thought: where to find
A bicycle to pedal there swifter?
Consider though, the plainness of moving.
Study the beauty of all that is slow.
Think on what unfathomably human
Condition defines our simple walking.
Nothing in life has helped us come and go
More than this joy allowed to every man.

19 February, 2015

Wayford Bridge to Great Yarmouth

Long unvisited and left neglected
Stays the town monument to Lord Nelson,
Greatest naval hero of Great Britain;
A dulled column as dilapidated
As the remnant of the close-by castle.
No things here are new, but worse still, nothing
Is used for anything, as everything
Rusts dormant in its static death cycle.
Spaces are closed. Those that survive open
Enclose empty voids of assembled grief
Where no-one speaks to nobody and brief
Scowls of woe serve for communication.
Gone are the days of Yarmouth's great glory:
What would Nelson say? *Kismet*, possibly.

20 February, 2015

Great Yarmouth to Lowestoft

Less than a year into my life, we moved
Athwart the world; from that fragrant harbour,
Famed Pearl of the Orient, out we flew
For a Western start in Australia.
After a childhood opened down under,
I grew adult outside that rich island
As I sailed West to see older wonders,
And sought the stars from Oz to Albion.
And now, I turn once more from East to West;
The way that I have wandered since my birth.
Ahead, a route of concluding roads wends
Ever nearer to a long-promised rest:
I walk against the spinning of the Earth,
Drawn towards sunset and my journey's end.

21 February, 2015

Lowestoft to Bungay

Health check: physically, things are okay.
My right knee seizes up on occasion
And both soles are really worn and roughened.
Happily, there's no real pain to allay,
Nothing chronic nor acute to prompt fear.
I've noticed though that I'm not quite walking
As quickly as I had been at starting:
The body's slowing down, that much is clear.
As for the mind, it's sharper than ever:
Questions appear and return in a stream
Of open thought beside uncluttered fields,
And each repetition refines clearer
The veiled litany of quiescent dreams
From which tender mysteries are revealed.

22 February, 2015

Bungay to Diss

There are places I know only by name,
Which exist, passed by, as formless stations
Or dark, unrecognised destinations
Bold displayed on roadside signs, with no claim
Within my heart: never were intentions
To explore these unknown localities,
Stilled as unexperienced memories
Waiting at the ends of roads not taken.
Of these cities to where I've never been,
Of untested and untasted graces,
I've some feeling that I've lived them before:
They seem just like past somewheres that I've seen,
Familiar and personal spaces
Still kept dear in my mind's eye and heart's core.

23 February, 2015

Diss to Bury St. Edmunds

I've been down on darkened and dirtied lanes,
Over snow-packed paths leading to high peaks,
Through slings and arrows of outrageous rains,
In a river muddied with silt-sludge streaks.
I've passed by thudding trucks set straight at me,
Across fields full of untamed animals,
Amid angry men swarmed as angry bees,
Near places of risks and near-missed perils.
I've gone out to strange centres of nowhere,
Further than I thought my feet could endure,
Further than I felt my spirit could bear,
Under mean clouds of tumult and thunder.
After such testing times, of this I'm sure:
I'm not scared of anything, anymore.

24 February, 2015

Bury St. Edmunds to Newmarket

That is it! One thousand miles! Done! Hurrah!
Yet this is no grand, champagne achievement;
Digits may count to four significant
Figures, but numbers simply mark how far
And farther. The additional zero
Is wholly empty of richer meaning;
A hollow integer that means nothing,
And of course, *nihil fit ex nihilo*.
Hid behind that third nought is a shaped 'o',
A circle balanced and substantial, vast
With single-stroke profundity and pure
In completeness: a numeric *ensō*
Of the present, which fences in a past
And leaves open an expansive future.

25 February, 2015

Newmarket to Cambridge

Only an hour ago I sat with soul
Enraptured under a fan vault sky arched
Above luminous panes of glass painted
Still and soft as a boy sang out his soul
In mellifluous treble voice and made
Hearts tremble in reverence to divine
Presence with each fond note sounding down time
Before a boy's youthful voice will soon fade
And break. Fading too fast also is my
Recollection as today's shapes and sounds
Are even now left to perfidious
Memory uncertain of times gone by
And although thoughts are regained and refound
The things that have been lost are most precious.

26 February, 2015

Cambridge to St. Neots

I walk out of this city of learning;
Away from a shared, inquisitive mind
Of the eager and erudite, turning
Over the great questions of humankind.
I remember how it all felt, to be
A part of this tradition, years ago
At the University of Sydney,
Sidere mens eadem mutato:
Scholarly world of research, discussion,
Proposition then counter-argument,
Belief in the value of invention,
And for a certain few, enlightenment.
I walk on, studied and solitary,
Long since detached from that community.

27 February, 2015

St. Neots to Bedford

It is an unexpected encounter:
Eyes search with uncertain recognition
Whilst mouths speak in fitful conversation,
With silent spaces that stretch still longer.
Old friends, both men wrestle to recover
The long interval of lost connection,
And share the same, unvoiced realisation
That they now stand strangers to each other.
Though faces have aged and voices ripened
Across lengthened years of separation,
This late moment of serendipity
Relights the lasted warmth of once-shortened
Friendship, then leaves the friends to reflection
And the delights of rediscovery.

28 February, 2015

Bedford to Stony Stratford

The man, whatever happened to the man?
The one who always appeared so content
Whilst in control of each working moment,
Checking daily tasks off his yearly plan.
First in at daybreak and last out at night,
He toiled away in his brown worsted suit;
An earnest employee of good repute,
Keen to make sure that all things were just right.
The boy hides in the whispers of his mind,
In every passing story that he tells
And all the actions that his soul compels;
Tapping at his heart, from front and behind.
Does the man still dare to dream, to explore?
Enough to grow into a boy once more?

1 March, 2015

Stony Stratford to Stowe

I know these streets, whence they come and whither
They run through these long-familiar fields;
These temples emblazoned with swords and shields,
And of stones and stories carved forever.
It is here that I have slept and much dreamt
In idle hours, then woke with life to live.
I find myself returned, ready to give
Back those stuffs which were once begun and spent.
Time circles ceaseless around clock faces,
As certain as the sun also rises
When night stars fall and dawn leads a new day.
What awaits our return to past places?
I come by the old roads and same guises;
But I arrive by a different way.

2 March, 2015

Stowe (again)

You are eager to get out there, so full of a teenager's enthusiasm
For fearless, intrepid exploration; to head off now to outlying lands where
Everything is caught in constant motion; to follow fortunes leading out to rare
Kingdoms beyond any and all compare; and to seek some sense of satisfaction
Out of the stories that you'll live to tell, of how you overcame countless dangers
In the course of your unbound adventures. You feel that school constrains you, from the bell
That tolls for this lesson and that lecture, to rules that confine, restrain and compel;
You wish to bid this school life farewell and to find one that is more free and greater.
I've seen a lot of the world in past days, and all the wonders and marvels have been
Worth the hurt of the experience. Do think more highly of your own innocence —
Education teaches those quiet things not seen: the knowledge, questions, means and ways
To understand what you see and survey; to grasp what you hear without and within.
Without schooling you lose a sense, remain less certain of what defines your presence;
You go into the world a blind and deaf teen, with all perspective in disarray.

3 March, 2015

69

Stowe (once more)

There is this secluded and shaded grove
Not easily noticed by passers-by
Where an ellipse of matured trees surround
An autumnal sea of long-fallen leaves
One tree stands solitary amidst all
A sapling rising slowly year on year
It is wintered bare to a slender trunk
Visibly without width and without leaf
Yet it is full with personal meaning
Each tiny branch a tender reminder
Of memories deep-rooted in the mind
This slight and single whip of English oak
Unknown and left alone by most others
Draws me back and back to this soulful space.

4 March, 2015

Stowe to Bicester

Two wide bowls of warm pasta are plated
With fresh asparagus and flaked salmon,
Served up for supper and soon digested
Alongside spirited conversation.
Next follows coffee and some collected
Tales of old days and new aspirations;
Then, at day's end, well-nourished and quite tired,
A soft bed grants rest and relaxation.
There is a taste of the ordinary
In this evening full of simple pleasure,
Spent in contented ease at the humble
Home of a friend, in friendly company.
Through these three months of erratic venture,
Comfort comes in what is plain and normal.

5 March, 2015

Bicester to Oxford

There seems no alternative way to pass.
The road is blocked with solid obstructions:
Wide traffic cones flank thick-set construction
Vehicles, herded in a bulky mass;
Workmen crowd out the remaining margins,
Hauling double-walled barriers over
The exposed roadside edges, to deter
Any and all likely shenanigans.
Though modest, the greatest grace of walking
Is that one can go wherever the mind
Wills and anywhere the body carries.
Helped along by some creative thinking,
Chance and benign trespass, one always finds
Shortcuts and sidetracks to such boundaries.

6 March, 2015

Oxford to Faringdon

I learnt well some verses of Tennyson
Years ago when noble dreams were begat;
Now older, I have remained hopeful that
Some work of noble note may yet be done.
If only there were still some time and cause
To follow knowledge like a sinking star;
To sail from here beyond sunsets afar,
Having tasted how dull it is to pause.
I wonder if I come too late to seek
A newer world of restored perspectives:
Each untraveled lane and uncharted field
Exhorts my equal-tempered heart to keep
Faith in that mantra of infinitives:
To strive, to seek, to find, and not to yield.

7 March, 2015

Faringdon to Wootton Bassett

We meet in the hotel foyer, faced at
A diagonal, as if two boxers
Glaring across at each other whilst sat,
He and I, broodingly in our corners.
They tell me, enthused, of his planned journey,
And already, they hail him a hero –
Six mere days through his itinerary
From England down to Kilimanjaro.
All know that my exploits are the lesser.
Between us, there is no semblance of talk
Despite our close-related endeavour:
I have my measure and he has his walk.
This is though, no distance competition;
Each man need seek his own inspiration.

8 March, 2015

Wootton Bassett to Corsham

People are always so very polite
To judge my small adventure arduous.
They think mistakenly of extreme heights
And all manner of dark and dangerous
Threats that lurk within a fairy-tale grove.
The reality is quite different:
No wilderness, no tent, no camping stove,
No roughing it, no mountainous ascent,
No need for packaged, dehydrated food;
Nights are spent in bedrooms at bland hotels,
Where expended energies are renewed,
All with neatly set soaps and shower gels.
I'm happy to be honest and to say
That it's all just a walking holiday.

9 March, 2015

Corsham to Frome

This morning, *The Times* listed thirty picks
For Britain's most fashionable places
To live. Here I am, sampling some graces
Recommended of number twenty-six.
What is the essence of 'fashionable'?
Hipster cafés, shops stocked with designer
Homewares, hotels dressed in chic furniture –
Do these things improve upon the 'normal'?
There was a time, some years ago, when I
Considered buying a cosy, stone-walled
House near here, and to relocate to Frome.
Homes were offered but I chose not to buy –
The market has since moved. Prices have soared
In this fashionable property boom.

10 March, 2015

Frome to Street

It was in that instant that our eyes met,
Caught in momentary indecision;
Like two star-crossed lovers, our course seemed set
Towards unavoidable collision.
I had foreseen and heard her approaching,
Long before she emerged at that blind bend;
But she did not notice me retreating
In key movements she failed to comprehend.
I shall remember her tense expression,
Those widened, frightened eyes with which she passed;
Her fleeted flash of rushed realisation
That she was moving ahead far too fast.
Thus she drove by, at high speed and on edge,
With me trapped tight against the roadside hedge.

11 March, 2015

Street to Ilminster

Gatsby floats in his pool without delight,
Then opens his eyes to sight George Wilson;
He reaches out once more for the green light
That marks his love for Daisy Buchanan.
Scout stands in Boo's shoes on the Radley porch,
Thinking of all that has passed, and of Tom;
She knows this is the end of childhood's torch
And last of such carefree days in Maycomb.
Old Man Santiago sleeps unaware,
His mind out at sea beside his marlin;
He wakes to a boy's affection and care
Before falling into his dreams again.
The past is so much struggle and sorrow;
Hope is always alive in tomorrow.

12 March, 2015

Ilminster to Honiton

There are a near-dozen charity shops,
Full of what were once somebody's treasures.
A newly-employed shop attendant mops
Round the piled junk of unwanted pleasures:
From oil portraits of unknown figures and
Hickory-shafted sand wedges and woods,
To sets of second-hand furniture and
Multifarious superfluous goods.
Farther up the road trade the antiques shops,
Each with postcard windows of old treasures:
From bureaux inlaid with various woods
And early twentieth-century mops,
To vintage toys of nostalgic pleasures –
Cast off chattels revamped as Veblen goods.

13 March, 2015

Honiton to Exeter

He chats, both informed and with intellect:
This younger man sitting alongside me
Tells his tales of nights spent with refugees,
Of dialogues in juggled dialects,
Of rough detours through countries and kingdoms
To which I am shamed never to have been,
But in which he has lived a time, and seen
The people wage war to win their freedoms.
I listen, and look into his wised eyes,
To see a man as master of his fears
And no slave to the sloth of ignorance.
The truth I have tonight come to realise
Is that a man ages not in his years,
But rather, out of his experience.

14 March, 2015

Exeter to Okehampton

The last of the hills recedes to the sea
And streams suffuse into the beaten earth;
In the liberty of equality
Prodigal sons return with righteous worth.
The rocks corrode in round coatings of rust
And the garden gates are soon to be closed;
In the dandelion drift is the dust
Of deep-rooted resentments decomposed.
The sun settles low on the horizon
And dusk frames the last edges of the day;
In the coarse winds of the changing season
Old desires dissolve to times far away.
Only a distance remains between here
And the end of things, somewhere over there.

15 March, 2015

Okehampton to Launceston

I exist alone at a nowhere place
Enclosed by nothing but the exposed air
Where nobody can notice me and where
No one can hear me in the soundless space
Of surrounds that are entirely empty
But for the shades of the sunken shadows
Held by the slow hugs of the hushed hollows
Wherein exists no entity but me
At a solitary nowhere I stand
As one unsighted and silently free
From seven billion other people
In the now I am become an island
And though the moment is momentary
There exists me in the ephemeral

16 March, 2015

Launceston to Liskeard

Best of friends laughing in quiet corners;
Loving mothers balancing cute babies
Carefully and tenderly on their knees;
Calm men perusing morning newspapers:
This is a place where everyone belongs,
Whether their choice is made for black or white,
For pulled or pressed, for dark, medium, light,
For single-origin, for short or long.
Meanwhile, a scientist cleans some glassware
For an exactingly pure filtration
In his specialist laboratory;
A sanctum where he carefully prepares
An alchemy of perfect extraction,
And serves up his superior coffee.

17 March, 2015

Liskeard to St. Austell

What is solid, quite like *rice*; which, after
Things have been liquefied, might almost seem
To be a rather strange looking *wafer*,
Boiled in a gaseous release of *dream*
That starts with saint, not doctor? Innately
An important part of both me and you,
This shapeless yet structural trinity
Is a stuff that can be renewed and new –
A substance constantly recycled. In
It, the start of all nature's life is found,
Whilst humans are stranded on land within
Its tied, concurrent and wavering bounds.
Still fishing around for the right answer?
Simply cast your hook into some water.

18 March, 2015

St. Austell to Truro

She has her ears blocked with coloured earplugs,
Whilst he stares blind at his telephone screen:
Old-fashioned good mornings, smiles, waves and hugs
Are consigned to the world of what has been.
Citizens walk quickly and hurry past
Strangers to shun any conversations:
Streets are crammed full with cars, driven too fast,
Without any care for pedestrians.
There are some cool youths who seem keen on talk,
But they spit their words in yammer and yap
That sound round grown-up ears like cheese and chalk:
Some might call this the generation gap.
Connections should stem from proximity,
Yet cities enhance anonymity.

19 March, 2015

Truro to Helston

Tomorrow is simply another sun
Added to what we have lived through today;
A logical step on a lifelong way,
Where some things are to come and some are done.
Despite my mind's late attempts to reason
My uncertainties, I lay awake, tense
And strangely uncontrolled in the suspense
Of night-before-dawn anticipation.
Do we know what shares of ourselves we keep
For tomorrow? Virtues of a soul's roar
Or vices disgraceful and ill-desired?
[*sigh*] The bed beckons me to restful sleep:
After all, my body is somewhat sore,
And I am, at this time, a little tired.

20 March, 2015

Helston to Lizard Point

So it is done: this lone exploration
– Of seventy-eight days, three pairs of shoes
And fourteen hundred miles – between and through
The extreme four points of mainland Britain.
Maybe, by a certain definition,
I might rightly claim that I, faithfully,
Have walked the length and breadth of the country.
What, you ask, *has been the greatest lesson?*
In life, in living, is so much to see
That the fundamental resolution
To Hamlet's famed existential question
Is unquestionably, 'To be'. *To be.*
You have been beside me in my walking:
Thank you, sincerely, for all your reading.

21 March, 2015

Route and Distance Chart

Day	Date	Route	Daily Mileage	Cumulative Mileage
1	January 3	Dunnet Head to Wick	23.0	23.0
2	January 4	Wick to Dunbeath	21.3	44.3
3	January 5	Dunbeath to Helmsdale	16.0	60.3
4	January 6	Helmsdale to Golspie	17.0	77.3
5	January 7	Golspie to Tain	16.7	94.0
6	January 8	Tain to Evanton	16.7	110.7
7	January 9	Evanton to Inverness	17.3	128.0
8	January 10	Inverness to Foyers	20.3	148.3
9	January 11	Foyers to Invergarry	21.0	169.3
10	January 12	Invergarry to Spean Bridge	15.5	184.8
11	January 13	Spean Bridge to Corran	18.5	203.3
12	January 14	Corran to Resipole	21.6	224.9
13	January 15	Resipole to Kilchoan	21.9	246.8
14	January 16	Kilchoan to Ardnamurchan Point to Kilchoan	11.6	258.4
15	January 17	Kilchoan to Resipole	21.9	280.3
16	January 18	Resipole to Corran	21.6	301.9
17	January 19	Corran to Kingshouse	19.7	321.6
18	January 20	Kingshouse to Crianlarich	23.9	345.5
19	January 21	Crianlarich to Tarbet	16.6	362.1
20	January 22	Tarbet to Balloch	16.6	378.7
21	January 23	Balloch to Strathblane	18.5	397.2
22	January 24	Strathblane to Falkirk	26.0	423.2
23	January 25	Falkirk to South Queensferry	24.0	447.2
24	January 26	South Queensferry to Edinburgh	12.1	459.3
25	January 27	Edinburgh to North Berwick	26.5	485.8
26	January 28	North Berwick to Dunbar	15.0	500.8
27	January 29	Dunbar to Eyemouth	20.6	521.4
28	January 30	Eyemouth to Belford	27.2	548.6
29	January 31	Belford to Alnwick	14.9	563.5
30	February 1	Alnwick to Morpeth	19.3	582.8
31	February 2	Morpeth to Newcastle	15.3	598.1
32	February 3	Newcastle to Durham	14.9	613.0
33	February 4	Durham to Darlington	18.6	631.6
34	February 5	Darlington to Northallerton	16.1	647.7
35	February 6	Northallerton to Easingwold	22.4	670.1
36	February 7	Easingwold to York	15.1	685.2
37	February 8	York to Selby	14.9	700.1
38	February 9	Selby to Thorne	14.8	714.9

Day	Date	Route	Daily Mileage	Cumulative Mileage
39	February 10	Thorne to Gainsborough	21.5	736.4
40	February 11	Gainsborough to Lincoln	17.7	754.1
41	February 12	Lincoln to Woodhall Spa	17.9	772.0
42	February 13	Woodhall Spa to Boston	18.2	790.2
43	February 14	Boston to Holbeach	14.1	804.3
44	February 15	Holbeach to King's Lynn	17.9	822.2
45	February 16	King's Lynn to Huntstanton	16.5	838.7
46	February 17	Huntstanton to Wells-next-the-Sea	22.0	860.7
47	February 18	Wells-next-the-Sea to Cromer	24.2	884.9
48	February 19	Cromer to Wayford Bridge	20.7	905.6
49	February 20	Wayford Bridge to Great Yarmouth	19.7	925.3
50	February 21	Great Yarmouth to Lowestoft	10.3	935.6
51	February 22	Lowestoft to Bungay	16.5	952.1
52	February 23	Bungay to Diss	17.9	970.0
53	February 24	Diss to Bury St. Edmunds	23.6	993.6
54	February 25	Bury St. Edmunds to Newmarket	15.0	1008.6
55	February 26	Newmarket to Cambridge	13.3	1021.9
56	February 27	Cambridge to St. Neots	18.8	1040.7
57	February 28	St. Neots to Bedford	17.0	1057.7
58	March 1	Bedford to Stony Stratford	21.4	1079.1
59	March 2	Stony Stratford to Stowe	10.3	1089.4
60	March 3	Stowe	0.0	1089.4
61	March 4	Stowe	0.0	1089.4
62	March 5	Stowe to Bicester	12.4	1101.8
63	March 6	Bicester to Oxford	14.1	1115.9
64	March 7	Oxford to Faringdon	17.9	1133.8
65	March 8	Faringdon to Wootton Bassett	20.7	1154.5
66	March 9	Wootton Bassett to Corsham	18.1	1172.6
67	March 10	Corsham to Frome	18.1	1190.7
68	March 11	Frome to Street	24.3	1215.0
69	March 12	Street to Ilminster	20.7	1235.7
70	March 13	Ilminster to Honiton	19.4	1255.1
71	March 14	Honiton to Exeter	18.0	1273.1
72	March 15	Exeter to Okehampton	22.9	1296.0
73	March 16	Okehampton to Launceston	20.2	1316.2
74	March 17	Launceston to Liskeard	17.9	1334.1
75	March 18	Liskeard to St. Austell	23.1	1357.2
76	March 19	St. Austell to Truro	15.5	1372.7
77	March 20	Truro to Helston	17.6	1390.3
78	March 21	Helston to Lizard Point	12.8	1403.1

About the Author

Tony Chan is a former football coach and schoolmaster, who spent many years teaching English and Latin at Stowe. In his late twenties, seeking a higher experience of life, he entered – as he playfully terms it himself – the 'adventuring phase' of his life: trekking up Mount Kilimanjaro and joining passels of pilgrims on the Camino de Santiago. These explorations were the foundation stones for his *Four Points* walk. Born in Hong Kong, raised in Australia and now settled in Britain, much of his work deals with the confluence of national identities. He is presently writing a series of stories centred on displaced individuals – perhaps to be completed after another pilgrimage, from London to Rome, whilst reviewing restaurants along the way.

OOT **EYEWEAR** PUBLISHING

EYEWEAR
20/20
PAMPHLET
SERIES

SHORTLISTED
FOR THE
MICHAEL
MARKS
PUBLISHERS'
AWARD 2015

BEN STAINTON EDIBLES
MEL PRYOR DRAWN ON WATER
MICHAEL BROWN UNDERSONG
MATT HOWARD THE ORGAN BOX
RACHAEL M NICHOLAS SOMEWHERE NEAR IN THE DARK
BETH TICHBORNE HUNGRY FOR AIR
GALE BURNS OPAL EYE
PIOTR FLORCZYK BAREFOOT
LEILANIE STEWART A MODEL ARCHAEOLOGIST
SHELLEY ROCHE-JACQUES RIPENING DARK
SAMANTHA JACKSON SMALL CRIES
V.A. SOLA SMITH ALMOST KID
GEORGE SZIRTES NOTES ON THE INNER CITY
JACK LITTLE ELSEWHERE
DAMILOLA ODELOLA LOST & FOUND
KEITH JARRETT I SPEAK HOME
JESSICA MAYHEW AMOK
JULIE MORRISSY I AM WHERE
MICHAEL NAGHTEN SHANKS YEAR OF THE INGÉNUE
ALICE WILLINGTON LONG AFTER LIGHTS OUT

EYEWEAR
AVIATOR
PAMPHLET
SERIES

ELIZABETH PARKER ANTINOPOLIS
CLAIRE WILLIAMSON SPLIT ENDS
PAUL DEATON BLACK KNIGHT

MORE TO COME...